It Makes No Sense!

By Stephen Rickard

Published in 2026 by
Norwood House Press
2544 Clinton Street
Buffalo, NY 14224

Printed in the United States of America

Library of Congress Cataloging-in-Publication Data:
Names: Rickard, Stephen, 1957-, author. | Atkins, Jill (Children's author).
Title: It makes no sense / by Stephen Rickard. Nomad life / by Jill Atkins.
Description: Buffalo, NY : Norwood House Press, 2026. | Series: Phonics all-stars: phase 5c
Identifiers: ISBN 9781978578357 (pbk.) | ISBN 9781978578364 (library bound) | ISBN 9781978578371 (ebook)
Subjects: LCSH: Reading–Phonetic method–Juvenile literature. | English language–Phonetics–Juvenile literature. | Senses and sensation–Juvenile literature. | Nomads–Juvenile literature.
Classification: LCC LB1573.3 R534 2026 | DDC 372.465–dc23

CPSIA compliance information: Batch #CW26NHP: For further information contact Norwood House Press at 1-800-237-9932.

Most creatures on our planet have five senses.

You know what these senses are – we use them every day.

Some creatures have extra senses – senses that humans don't have. They can "see," or detect, things that are invisible to us.

Most people know about **bats**.

Bats can make a high-pitched clicking sound. The noise they make reflects back off objects, and the bats can "see" in the dark by listening to these sounds.

Electric eels have a different extra sense. They can detect fish that are near them in the water, using electrical sensors on their bodies.

The eels can give out electric shocks as well. When they have detected a fish, they can emit a shock to stun it.

Then it's lunchtime!

The **platypus** is quite an odd animal. It is a mammal, like us, but it has a bill (like a duck) and lays eggs (like a bird or a reptile).

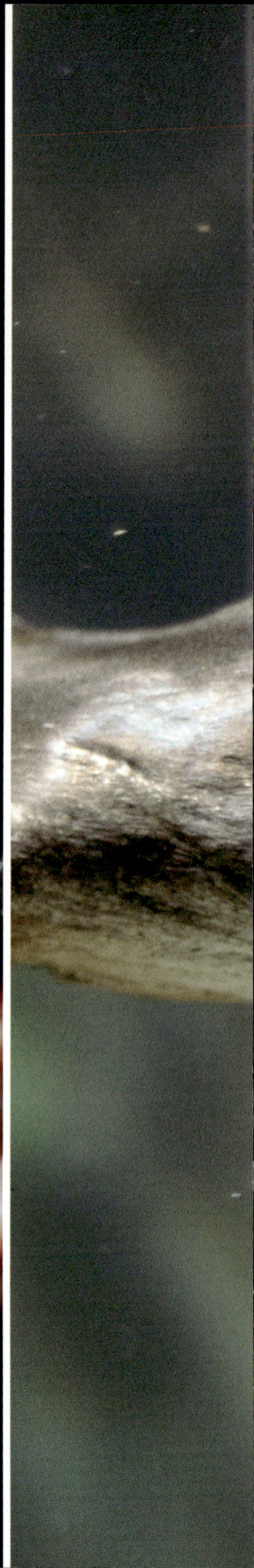

When a platypus dives to feed, it closes its eyes, nose, and ears. Then it finds its prey by detecting electric currents that the prey gives off.

It's rather like how electric eels do it but, with the platypus, it's a bit different.

This kind of snake is a **pit viper**.

Can you see the pits on its head next to its eyes and nostrils? In fact, the pits look like an extra pair of nostrils.

These pits can see infra-red light, which is light that we cannot see. In fact, it is not light but heat.

The pit viper can see the heat given off by an animal. So, if a mouse is hiding in the grass, the pit viper will still be able to see it.

Some **birds** can detect the magnetic forces on our planet.

They use them to find their way home when there are no clues to help them.

Some fish can do this too, as well as bats, frogs, lobsters, and bees.

These bugs are living fire-detectors. The bugs like to lay their eggs in trees that have been burned by fire.

So they can detect a forest fire up to 50 miles away. They will then fly to the fire to lay their eggs.

We must include spiders in this book too. Do spiders have a "spidey sense?"

Yes, they do. A spider has hairs on its body that can detect tiny changes around it. It can tell if an insect is trapped in its web, how big it is, and where it is.

So yes, a spider is a little hero.

Nomad Life

By Jill Atkins

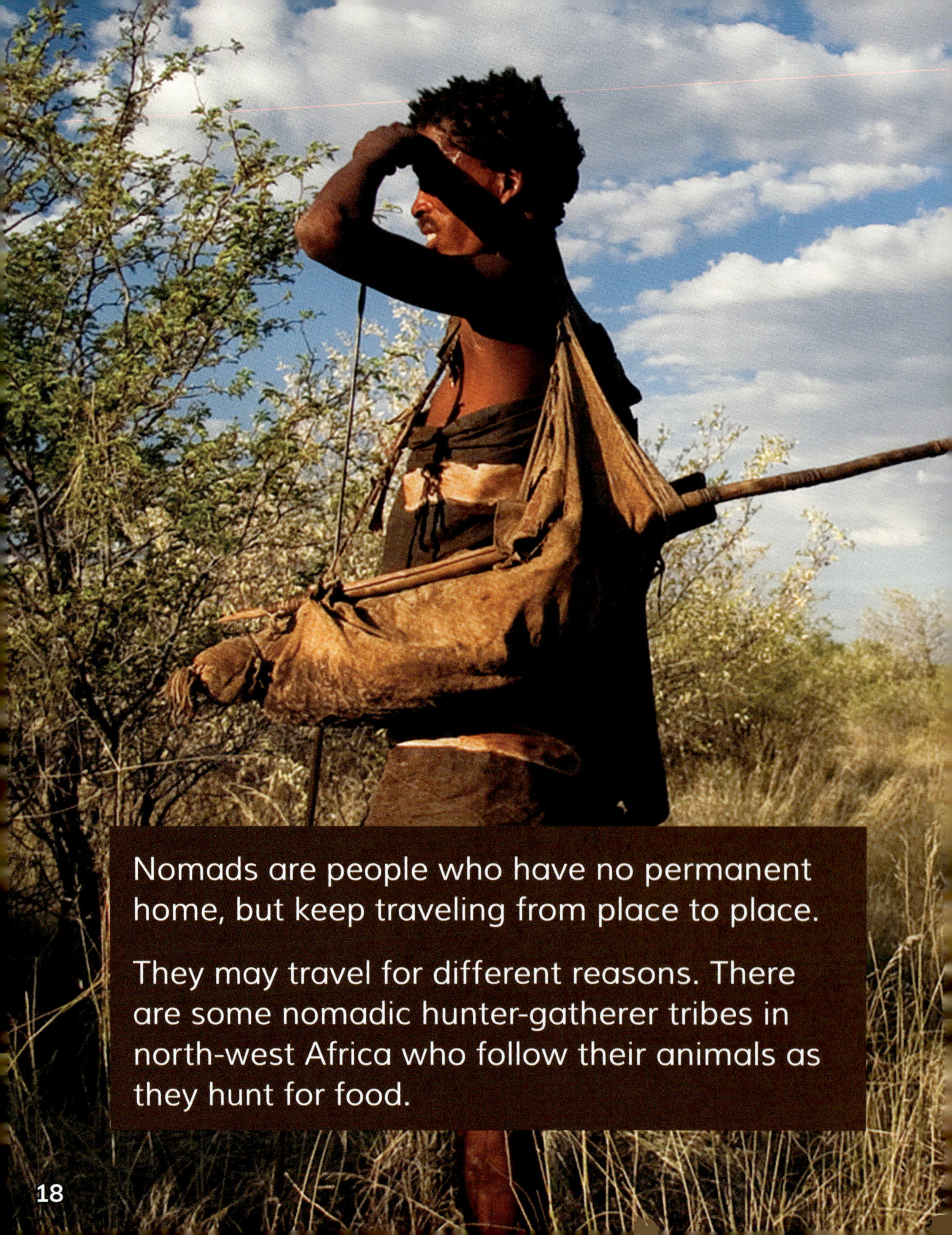

Nomads are people who have no permanent home, but keep traveling from place to place.

They may travel for different reasons. There are some nomadic hunter-gatherer tribes in north-west Africa who follow their animals as they hunt for food.

The land around them is very dry. Much of it is desert.

When there is nothing to eat, the people and their animals must travel, or they would starve.

Some North African nomads herd goats. Others have camels.

This is a camel train. The camels can carry quite heavy loads.

Some desert nomads live in tents like these. They carry the tents around with them.

In the Arctic, nomadic peoples live in freezing surroundings for many months of the year.

They need thick clothing made of animal skin.

This picture, which is one hundred years old, shows an igloo being constructed.

In past times, the men (and their sons) would leave and go hunting for many days.

For shelter, they would construct an igloo to keep out the freezing winds. They could even light a little fire inside the igloo.

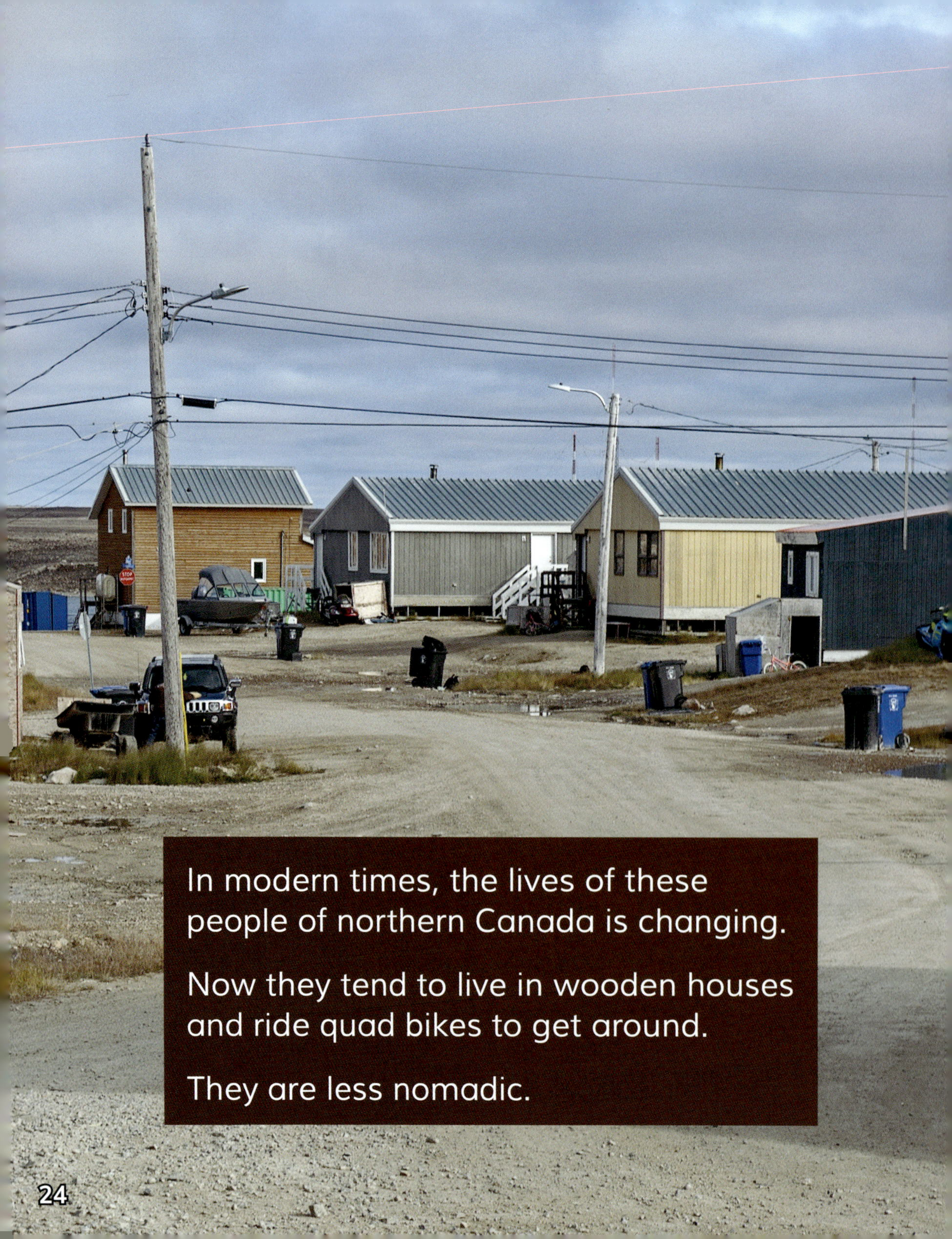

In modern times, the lives of these people of northern Canada is changing.

Now they tend to live in wooden houses and ride quad bikes to get around.

They are less nomadic.

These nomads live in Lapland, which is part of Arctic Norway, Sweden, and Finland.

These people travel on dog sleds, but sometimes these bigger animals pull them along.

Like all nomads, these people come and go with the seasons, using what they can find at different times of the year.

This man is feeding his animals.

1546 REINFOR

There are nomadic people in many other lands. They all have one thing in common – they all travel about, staying a few days, a few weeks, or even months in one place.

Some nomadic people live in big tents like these. They are called yurts.

These are old traveler caravans.

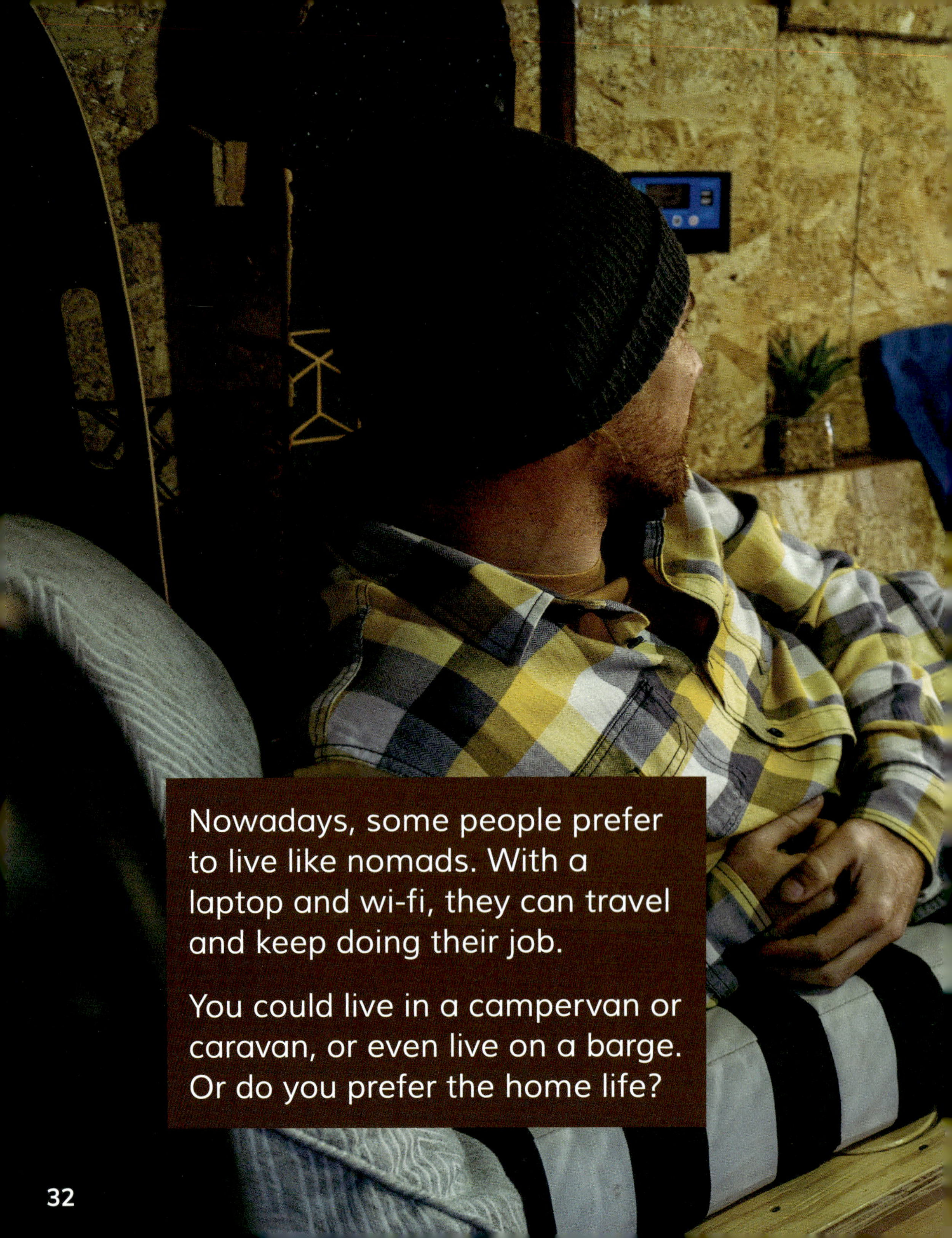

Nowadays, some people prefer to live like nomads. With a laptop and wi-fi, they can travel and keep doing their job.

You could live in a campervan or caravan, or even live on a barge. Or do you prefer the home life?